I0012610

Samsung Galaxy S24 Ultra User Guide

Unveiling the Galaxy S24 Ultra: The Ultimate Smartphone

By

Liam Vector

Disclaimer

This guidebook is intended for educational purposes only. It is not affiliated with, sponsored by, or endorsed by Samsung Electronics or any of its subsidiaries. The content within this book is based on publicly available information and personal research regarding the Samsung Galaxy S24 Ultra. The purpose of this guide is to provide a comprehensive, informative resource for users seeking to better understand the features, functionality, and usage of the device. It is not designed to promote or sell the product in any way.

Table of Contents

Chapter One

Introduction to the Samsung Galaxy S24 Ultra

1.1 Overview of the Samsung Galaxy S24 Ultra

The Samsung Galaxy S24 Ultra is one of the newest smartphones made by Samsung. It is a part of their Galaxy S series, which is known for offering top-notch technology and features. This phone is considered a flagship model, which means it is designed to be the best Samsung has to offer in terms of performance, design, and features.

The S24 Ultra is not just an ordinary phone. It comes with a variety of exciting upgrades and features that are meant to make using your phone smoother, faster, and more enjoyable. Whether you like to take great photos, watch high-quality videos, or play games, this phone is built to handle all of that. It's packed with a big screen, powerful processor, and some impressive camera technology.

At first glance, the Samsung Galaxy S24 Ultra may look like its predecessor, but when you take a closer look, you'll find many improvements that set it apart.

It combines design, performance, and functionality in a way that suits a wide range of users, from casual users to tech enthusiasts.

1.2 Key Features and Specifications

The Samsung Galaxy S24 Ultra comes with several features and specifications that make it stand out from the rest. Here's a simple breakdown of its most important features:

1. **Display**:
   The phone has a large 6.8-inch screen, which uses a technology called Dynamic AMOLED 2X. This screen is bright, sharp, and colorful. It also has a refresh rate that can change from 1Hz to 120Hz depending on what you are doing, making the phone feel smooth when you scroll or play games.

2. **Camera**:
   The S24 Ultra is equipped with an impressive 200-megapixel main camera. This camera allows you to take extremely detailed photos. There are also two telephoto cameras that help you zoom in on subjects without losing clarity. If you like taking wide-angle pictures

or selfies, the phone has cameras designed to handle those as well.

3. **Processor**:
   Inside the S24 Ultra, there's a powerful Qualcomm Snapdragon 8 Gen 3 processor. This makes the phone very fast and able to handle multiple tasks at once. Whether you're gaming or using several apps, the phone stays responsive and smooth.

4. **Battery**:
   The S24 Ultra comes with a big 5,000 mAh battery. This means the phone can last throughout the day without needing to be charged, even with heavy use. It also supports fast charging, so you can get your battery charged up quickly when needed.

5. **Storage**:
   The phone is available in three different storage options: 256GB, 512GB, and 1TB. This gives users plenty of space to store apps, photos, videos, and other files.

6. **S Pen**:
   The Galaxy S24 Ultra comes with a built-in S Pen, a stylus that allows you to write, draw,

and interact with your phone in unique ways. This is perfect for users who like to take notes, create artwork, or navigate the phone with precision.

7. **5G Connectivity**:
   The S24 Ultra supports 5G, which means it can connect to faster internet networks for downloading, streaming, and browsing the web.

8. **Operating System**:
   The phone runs on Android 14 with Samsung's custom skin called One UI. This skin gives users a smooth and personalized experience with a variety of extra features not found on other Android phones.

1.3 What's New in the Galaxy S24 Ultra?

The Galaxy S24 Ultra is packed with new features that make it a big improvement over previous models. Here are some of the most notable updates:

1. **Improved Camera System**:
   One of the biggest upgrades in the S24 Ultra

is its camera system. Samsung has added a 200-megapixel main camera, which is a significant improvement over the previous models. This new camera system allows users to take clearer, more detailed photos, even in low light. The S24 Ultra also has enhanced zoom capabilities, so you can get closer to your subjects without losing quality.

2. **AI Features**:
   Samsung has incorporated artificial intelligence (AI) into the S24 Ultra to improve its camera and overall performance. For example, AI helps the camera choose the best settings for your photos, making them look better without any extra effort from the user. The phone can also learn your habits and optimize performance based on how you use it.

3. **Faster Performance**:
   Thanks to the Snapdragon 8 Gen 3 processor, the S24 Ultra is faster than earlier models. This processor allows the phone to run demanding apps and games without slowing down. It also improves energy efficiency, meaning the phone can run longer on a single charge.

4. **Enhanced Display**:
   The S24 Ultra's display has improved color accuracy and brightness compared to previous models. The phone also has a more adaptive refresh rate, which adjusts based on what you are doing. For example, when watching videos, the refresh rate increases for smoother playback, while when reading or browsing the web, it slows down to save battery.

5. **Design Refinements**:
   While the S24 Ultra looks similar to its predecessors, it has received a few design tweaks that make it feel more premium. The phone's body is thinner, and the camera module has been redesigned to look sleeker. These small changes make the phone more comfortable to hold and more attractive to look at.

6. **Battery and Charging**:
   The battery life has been improved with better power management, and it can charge faster than previous models. This means you can get more use out of the phone without having to charge it constantly.

7. **New S Pen Features**:
    The built-in S Pen has been upgraded with new features that make it even more useful. For example, the S Pen can now be used for remote control functions, such as taking photos from a distance or navigating through apps. This makes the S Pen more versatile and a useful tool for anyone who needs to be productive.

8. **Better Software Features**:
    Samsung's One UI has been updated with new features that make the phone easier to use and more customizable. For instance, the phone has better multitasking capabilities, so you can easily switch between apps and use them side by side.

Chapter Two

Design and Build

2.1 Display: The 6.8-inch Dynamic AMOLED 2X

The Samsung Galaxy S24 Ultra comes with a big, bright screen called a **6.8-inch Dynamic AMOLED 2X** display. When you first look at the phone, the display is one of the first things you will notice because it looks very clear and colorful. Let's break down why this screen is special.

A screen's job is to show things clearly, so the Galaxy S24 Ultra uses AMOLED technology. AMOLED stands for **Active Matrix Organic Light Emitting Diode**, which is just a fancy way of saying that each little part of the screen (called a pixel) can light up individually. This helps the display show deeper blacks and more vibrant colors compared to older screens. This is why when you watch videos or look at pictures, everything looks rich and colorful. It makes everything you see on the screen come to life in a way that you can enjoy every detail.

One of the standout features of the display is **Dynamic AMOLED 2X**. This term refers to a few improvements over regular AMOLED screens. First, the "2X" part means that the screen is much brighter and clearer, even in bright sunlight. This makes the phone easy to use outdoors, where the sun might make other screens hard to see. If you enjoy watching videos or playing games, the brightness is important because it helps you see everything clearly, even in the sun.

Also, the **Dynamic AMOLED 2X** display has an adaptive refresh rate. What this means is that the phone can adjust the smoothness of the screen depending on what you are doing. For example, when you're scrolling through social media or browsing the internet, the screen refreshes at a lower rate to save battery. But, when you're playing games or watching fast-moving videos, the refresh rate increases to make the images on the screen move smoothly, without any jerky movement. This helps you have a better experience when you're using your phone.

The screen is **6.8 inches** in size, which makes it quite large. This is perfect if you like big screens for watching movies, playing games, or multitasking. It provides you with plenty of space to see and do everything. The screen's size makes it comfortable to read articles or watch videos without feeling cramped.

The **resolution** of the display is very high, meaning that the picture you see on the screen is extremely sharp. With high resolution, you can see small details in images or text clearly. Whether you're looking at photos or reading an article, everything appears crisp and precise.

Lastly, the Galaxy S24 Ultra's screen is made of **Corning Gorilla Glass Victus 2**, which is one of the strongest types of glass used in smartphones. This helps protect the screen from scratches and cracks if the phone is dropped.

2.2 Materials and Durability

The materials used to make the Samsung Galaxy S24 Ultra are chosen carefully to make the phone durable and strong, while also looking good. The back of the phone is made of **glass**, and the frame is made of **aluminum**. Both of these materials are used because they make the phone feel solid in your hand, while also keeping it light enough to carry around.

The front of the phone is covered by **Gorilla Glass Victus 2**, which is a tough type of glass. This is one of the toughest materials available for phone screens. It helps protect the screen from everyday bumps and drops, so you don't need to worry too much if the phone falls to the ground. The glass used here is also resistant to scratches, which means it will stay looking new for a longer time, even if you put it in your pocket with keys or other objects.

The frame of the phone is made from **aluminum**, which is both strong and lightweight. Aluminum is a great material because it adds strength to the phone without making it too heavy. The frame holds everything together securely and ensures that the phone doesn't bend easily. It also gives the phone a premium feel when you hold it.

The **back** of the phone, which you may touch while holding it, is also made of glass. This glass is smooth to the touch and gives the phone a shiny, polished look. However, glass can also be slippery, which means it may be a little easier to drop the phone if you're not careful. To fix this, many people use phone cases to add a grip and protect the glass from cracks or scratches.

The materials used for the Galaxy S24 Ultra are also chosen for their **durability**. While glass is strong, it can still break if dropped from a great height, but the overall build of the phone is designed to protect the screen and other parts. The aluminum frame around the glass helps absorb some of the impact if you drop it.

One of the important things to note is that the phone has an **IP68 water and dust resistance rating**. This means the phone is resistant to both dust and water. You can take the Galaxy S24 Ultra outside on a rainy day without worrying about water damage. It can also survive being submerged in water for a short period of time, making it great for outdoor use or if you accidentally spill water on it.

The materials and build quality of the Samsung Galaxy S24 Ultra are designed not only to look good but also to last. The phone is sturdy and strong, and the materials used help keep it safe from everyday wear and tear. If you take care of the phone, it should last for a long time without any major issues.

2.3 Handling and Comfort

When you pick up the Samsung Galaxy S24 Ultra, it feels solid but not too heavy. The size of the phone can feel a little large for some people, but the weight is balanced, and it doesn't feel too light or too heavy. The glass back is smooth, and the aluminum frame makes it feel premium in your hand. The phone feels like it's made well and not flimsy, which is important when you're using it every day.

Even though the phone is large with its 6.8-inch display, Samsung has designed it in a way that it's still comfortable to hold. The edges of the phone are rounded, not sharp, so it doesn't dig into your hand when you hold it. This is important because a phone that's too sharp or uncomfortable can be hard to use for long periods of time.

However, because the phone is large, it can be a bit challenging to use with one hand, especially if you have smaller hands. You might find yourself stretching your fingers to reach the top of the screen, which can be a little awkward. For people with smaller hands, this could be a concern, but Samsung includes features in the phone that can help, like one-handed mode, which makes the screen smaller and easier to use.

The glass back, while smooth, can sometimes make the phone slippery to hold. If you're worried about dropping it, you might want to use a **phone case**. Cases can add grip and help protect the phone from accidental falls. A case can also protect the phone from scratches or cracks if it falls.

The phone's buttons are placed at convenient spots. The **volume buttons** and **power button** are on the right side of the phone, making them easy to reach when holding the phone in your right hand. The **USB-C charging port** is at the bottom of the phone, and the **SIM card slot** is on the left side. These locations make it easy to use the phone without struggling to reach certain buttons or ports.

The **curved edges** of the display give it a modern look, but they can also make it a bit tricky when you're trying to hold the phone in a specific way, especially when it's lying flat on a surface. The curved edge can sometimes cause accidental touches on the screen, which can be annoying. However, you can adjust the settings to reduce this issue, such as turning on features that prevent accidental touches on the edge.

Finally, despite its large size, the Galaxy S24 Ultra is still **pocketable** for many people. If you like to carry your phone in your pocket, it might fit comfortably, but if you're wearing tight pants or a small pocket, you might find it difficult to fit. Using a larger bag or case can help if you find it a bit too large for your pockets.

Conclusion

The design and build quality of the Samsung Galaxy S24 Ultra are carefully crafted to provide a premium experience. From its large, bright display to its durable materials and comfortable handling, the phone is designed to stand out and perform well. Whether you're using it for work, play, or everything in between, the S24 Ultra is built to impress. While the phone's size can be challenging for some users, it's made to feel comfortable and sturdy in your hands, with features that protect it from damage. With its high-quality materials and strong build, the Galaxy S24 Ultra is made to last.

Chapter Three

Performance and Software

3.1 Qualcomm Snapdragon 8 Gen 3 Chipset

The Qualcomm Snapdragon 8 Gen 3 chipset is one of the most important parts of the Samsung Galaxy S24 Ultra. It acts like the brain of the phone, helping it to run apps, games, and tasks smoothly and quickly. To make it easier to understand, think of the Snapdragon 8 Gen 3 as the engine of a car. The engine helps the car move, and in the same way, the Snapdragon chipset helps the phone run all the things you want to do.

Snapdragon 8 Gen 3 is a **powerful processor**, meaning it can handle multiple tasks at the same time without slowing down. Whether you are watching videos, using social media, or playing games, this processor makes sure everything runs smoothly. It can do all these things faster than previous processors, which is one reason the Samsung Galaxy S24 Ultra feels quick and responsive.

This chipset has been built to handle **advanced tasks**, such as **AI (Artificial Intelligence)** and **machine learning**. For example, when you use the camera, the

Snapdragon 8 Gen 3 can automatically make your photos look better by adjusting colors and brightness. It can also help the phone recognize faces in pictures and suggest ways to improve the photo before you even take it.

One of the best things about the Snapdragon 8 Gen 3 is that it is **energy-efficient**. This means the phone doesn't use too much power, even when you are using it a lot. So, the phone lasts longer on a single charge, which is great for people who need their phone to last all day without needing a recharge.

In simple terms, the Snapdragon 8 Gen 3 makes the Samsung Galaxy S24 Ultra fast, smart, and long-lasting. It ensures the phone works smoothly for everyday use and even when you are doing more complex tasks, like gaming or using heavy apps.

3.2 RAM, Storage, and Multitasking

When we talk about **RAM** (Random Access Memory), we are talking about the phone's ability to keep things open and running. If you've ever used a phone and tried to switch between apps, and it was slow to do so, it might have had too little RAM. RAM is like the short-term memory of the phone, helping it to quickly access apps and data while you are using them.

The Samsung Galaxy S24 Ultra comes with **12GB of RAM** (depending on the model you choose), which is a lot of RAM for a smartphone. With this amount of RAM, you can open many apps at once without worrying about the phone slowing down. For example, you can have a social media app, a web browser, and a game running in the background at the same time. The phone will keep all of these apps ready for you to use without having to reload them every time you switch between them. This is called **multitasking**, and with 12GB of RAM, the Galaxy S24 Ultra can handle it effortlessly.

Next, let's talk about **storage**. The Galaxy S24 Ultra comes in different storage sizes, ranging from **256GB** to **1TB**. The storage is where all your data, like apps, photos, music, and videos, are saved. The more storage you have, the more you can store on the phone without running out of space.

If you like to take lots of photos or download movies, you'll need a lot of storage. But don't worry, even with 256GB of storage, you'll have plenty of space for most people's needs. If you need more, the phone also comes with the 512GB and 1TB options, which provide even more space to keep all your files.

Storage on the Galaxy S24 Ultra is also **fast**. This means that when you open apps or save files, the process happens quickly. The phone's storage is built with a technology called **UFS 4.0**. This technology ensures that the data can be read and written very fast, so the phone runs smoothly.

Together, the large **RAM** and **fast storage** make the Samsung Galaxy S24 Ultra an excellent phone for multitasking. Whether you're switching between apps or saving lots of files, the phone can handle it without slowing down.

3.3 One UI and Software Features

The **One UI** is Samsung's custom version of the Android operating system. Think of Android like the foundation of the phone, and One UI is like the house built on top of that foundation. One UI makes the phone easier to use by adding extra features and making the phone look and feel unique.

One of the key features of One UI is its **user-friendly interface**. The phone's screen is large, but One UI makes it easy to use. It arranges apps and settings in a way that is simple to access, even on a big screen. For example, One UI allows you to move things around on the screen to make the most of the space, and it even has a **one-handed mode** for people who find the phone too big to use with just one hand.

Another useful feature is **Edge Panels**. This is a feature that allows you to access your most-used apps and tools quickly by swiping from the edge of the screen. You can customize the Edge Panels to show the apps, contacts, or tools you use the most, making them easier to reach without having to go to the home screen.

Dark Mode is another popular feature in One UI. When you turn on Dark Mode, the screen's background turns black, and the text becomes white. This not only looks cool, but it also helps save battery power because dark backgrounds use less energy on an AMOLED screen. It can also be easier on the eyes, especially if you're using the phone in low light.

One UI also includes many **security features** to keep your data safe. **Samsung Knox** is built into the phone, and it helps protect your personal information from hackers and other threats. There is also **biometric security**, such as **fingerprint scanning** and **facial**

recognition, which allows you to unlock the phone easily and securely.

Another cool feature is **Samsung DeX**. Samsung DeX allows you to connect the Galaxy S24 Ultra to a larger screen, such as a TV or computer monitor, and use the phone like a desktop computer. This is great if you want to do tasks like work on documents or watch videos on a bigger screen.

In short, One UI is what makes the Samsung Galaxy S24 Ultra unique. It adds extra features, makes the phone easy to use, and helps you customize the phone to fit your needs.

3.4 Gaming and Performance Benchmarks

The Samsung Galaxy S24 Ultra is not just a phone for everyday tasks like texting and calling. It's also a phone that can handle **gaming** and other high-performance tasks.

When it comes to gaming, the Snapdragon 8 Gen 3 chipset and 12GB of RAM come together to deliver a **smooth gaming experience**. Games that are graphically demanding, such as action-packed games or 3D games, run smoothly on the Galaxy S24 Ultra.

You won't experience lag or stuttering while playing, and the phone keeps the graphics looking sharp and detailed. The large display makes games look even better, and the fast refresh rate ensures that the movement on screen is smooth.

Samsung also has a feature called **Game Launcher**. This feature helps manage and optimize your gaming experience. It puts all your games in one place, making it easy to find and open them. Game Launcher also has a **Game Tools** menu that allows you to adjust settings while playing. For example, you can block notifications so that you don't get interrupted, or you can adjust the game's performance settings to save battery life.

To measure how well the Samsung Galaxy S24 Ultra performs, we look at **performance benchmarks**. Benchmarks are tests that measure how well a phone can handle tasks like gaming, app usage, and multitasking. The Galaxy S24 Ultra performs very well in these benchmarks, meaning it's a **top-performing phone**. The phone scores high in both **single-core** (tasks that use just one part of the processor) and **multi-core** (tasks that use multiple parts of the processor) tests. This shows that the phone is fast and capable of handling both simple tasks and complex ones without slowing down.

The phone's **gaming performance** is also impressive. Whether you're playing fast-paced action games or graphically intense games, the Samsung Galaxy S24 Ultra's hardware can keep up. The screen's high refresh rate, paired with the powerful chipset, creates a **great gaming experience**, with no lag or freezing.

For those who want to take mobile gaming to the next level, the Galaxy S24 Ultra is ready. You can enjoy all your favorite games, from simple puzzle games to detailed action games, with smooth performance and beautiful graphics.

Conclusion

In this chapter, we have covered the performance and software features of the Samsung Galaxy S24 Ultra. From the powerful **Snapdragon 8 Gen 3 chipset** that makes the phone fast and efficient to the **One UI** software that enhances the Android experience, this phone is built to handle everything you want to do. Whether you're multitasking, playing games, or using apps, the Galaxy S24 Ultra delivers smooth performance. The 12GB of RAM and high storage options ensure that you can store all your data without worrying about running out of space. Plus, the gaming experience is top-notch, with powerful hardware that handles the latest games with ease.

The Samsung Galaxy S24 Ultra offers a well-rounded experience for people who want a high-performance phone. Whether you're using it for work, play, or both, this phone has everything you need to get the job done.

Chapter Four

The Camera System

The camera system in the Samsung Galaxy S24 Ultra is one of its standout features. It offers an impressive combination of cameras that help you capture photos and videos in excellent quality. This chapter will guide you through all the important camera features, including how to use them and what makes them so great.

4.1 200MP Primary Camera: Details and Features

The **200MP primary camera** is the star of the camera system on the Galaxy S24 Ultra. In simple terms, this means the main camera can capture **200 million tiny details** in every photo. Imagine a picture made up of millions of small dots, and the more dots there are, the clearer and sharper the image will be.

This **200MP camera** is special because it allows you to take **incredibly detailed photos**. Even when you zoom in on a photo, the details stay sharp. This is useful when you want to capture small objects or distant subjects and still see everything clearly.

Now, you might wonder, why is 200MP important? Most smartphones have cameras with far fewer megapixels. For example, many phones have 12MP or 48MP cameras. The higher the number of megapixels, the better the camera can capture fine details, and with the Galaxy S24 Ultra, you get a **200MP camera**, which is among the best available.

One of the great features of the 200MP camera is that it uses **pixel binning**. Pixel binning is a process where the camera combines multiple pixels into one large pixel. This helps make photos look clearer, especially in low light. Instead of capturing blurry pictures when it's dark, the 200MP camera combines pixels to capture better quality images.

The **autofocus** feature also makes this camera super smart. It can quickly focus on the subject of the photo, whether it's a person, animal, or object, making sure everything in the picture is sharp and clear.

In short, the **200MP primary camera** is fantastic for taking super-detailed photos. It's great for both bright and dark settings, thanks to its ability to combine pixels and improve quality.

4.2 Telephoto and Periscope Lenses

In addition to the 200MP primary camera, the Samsung Galaxy S24 Ultra also comes with **telephoto and periscope lenses**. These lenses are used for zooming in on subjects from far away without losing image quality.

- **Telephoto Lens**: The telephoto lens on the Galaxy S24 Ultra helps you zoom in on subjects up to **3x optical zoom**. This means you can take a closer photo of something far away without actually having to get closer. For example, if you're at a concert or event, and you can't get close to the stage, you can use the telephoto lens to take clear pictures from far away.

- **Periscope Lens**: The **periscope lens** is even more powerful than the telephoto lens. It offers **10x optical zoom**. This means you can zoom in even more, taking clear, sharp photos from a great distance. It's perfect for subjects that are far away, like animals in the wild or distant buildings.

Both of these lenses are designed to zoom in **optically**, meaning the camera physically adjusts the lens to zoom, instead of just digitally cropping the image. **Optical zoom** keeps the quality of the image intact, while **digital zoom** can make photos blurry when you zoom in too far.

Thanks to the telephoto and periscope lenses, you can take sharp and detailed photos even when you're far away from your subject. This is especially useful for wildlife photography, sporting events, or capturing distant landmarks.

4.3 Ultra-Wide and Front Camera

The Samsung Galaxy S24 Ultra doesn't just have a primary camera and zoom lenses. It also has an **ultra-wide camera** and a **front camera** that are both great for different types of photos.

- **Ultra-Wide Camera**: The **ultra-wide camera** is designed for capturing more of the scene. If you want to take a picture of a large group of people or a beautiful landscape, the ultra-wide camera is perfect. Instead of capturing just a narrow portion of the scene, it captures a much wider area. This is great for travel photos, group shots, or pictures where you want to include a lot of background, such as mountain ranges or cityscapes.

- **Front Camera (Selfie Camera)**: The **front camera** is used for taking selfies or video calls. The Galaxy S24 Ultra has a **12MP front camera**, which means it can take good-quality selfies with clear details. It also has a wide field of view, so you can fit more people in your selfie shot without anyone being left out. The front camera can also be used for **portrait mode**, which blurs the background and focuses on the person in front of the camera, making them look even more sharp and clear.

Both the ultra-wide and front cameras are perfect for **different types of photos**, whether you want to capture a large area, take a great selfie, or fit more people in your shot. They add a lot of versatility to the camera system, so you're ready for any kind of photo opportunity.

4.4 Camera Tips and Tricks

Now that we know about the main camera features, let's go over a few **camera tips and tricks** to help you get the best photos with your Galaxy S24 Ultra.

1. **Use Night Mode**: The **Night Mode** helps you take better photos in low light. If you're in a dimly lit place or outside at night, turn on Night Mode. It uses special settings to brighten up the photo and capture more details, so your pictures won't be too dark.

2. **Take Advantage of Portrait Mode**: Portrait Mode blurs the background and makes the subject of the photo stand out. It's great for taking photos of people, pets, or even flowers. If you want your photos to look more professional, use Portrait Mode.

3. **Use the Zoom Lenses Carefully**: The **telephoto and periscope lenses** are great for zooming in on distant subjects. But remember, if you zoom too much, it might be harder to keep the picture steady. To get clear pictures, try using a tripod or steady your hands when you're taking a zoomed-in shot.

4. **Play Around with Pro Mode**: If you want more control over your camera settings, try **Pro**

Mode. This allows you to adjust things like exposure, ISO, and shutter speed. If you're not sure how to use Pro Mode, don't worry. There are tutorials in the camera app to help guide you through it.

5. **Use the Ultra-Wide Camera for Large Scenes**: If you're taking pictures of landscapes or large groups, switch to the **ultra-wide camera**. It captures more of the scene, so nothing gets left out. Just remember that ultra-wide shots can sometimes look distorted at the edges, so try to focus on the center of the scene.

6. **Try the Super Steady Video Mode**: When you're recording videos, try using **Super Steady** mode. This feature helps smooth out shaky videos, so your footage will look stable and clear, even if you're moving around while filming.

7. **Experiment with the Camera Filters**: The camera app has many filters that can change the look of your photos. If you want to add a fun effect, try out the different filters. They can give your photos a creative touch, and you can always adjust the intensity of the filter to

get the perfect look.

4.5 Photo and Video Quality Review

Now that we've learned about the camera features and tips, let's talk about the **photo and video quality** you can expect from the Galaxy S24 Ultra.

- **Photo Quality**: The Galaxy S24 Ultra's photos are sharp, detailed, and vibrant. Whether you're using the 200MP primary camera, the ultra-wide camera, or the telephoto lenses, your photos will look clear, even when zoomed in. Thanks to the powerful camera system and features like **Night Mode** and **Pro Mode**, you can capture stunning images in any lighting condition. Whether you're indoors or outdoors, day or night, the camera works hard to make sure your photos look great.

- **Video Quality**: The video quality on the Galaxy S24 Ultra is also top-notch. It can record **4K and 8K video**, which means your videos will be incredibly clear and detailed. Whether you're filming a landscape, a concert, or a family event, the video quality will impress. The **Super Steady** mode helps keep your videos smooth, even when you're walking or moving around. The camera can also switch between lenses while recording, so you can zoom in and out without interrupting the video.

Overall, the photo and video quality of the Galaxy S24 Ultra is outstanding. It's perfect for anyone who loves taking pictures and videos, whether you're a beginner or an expert photographer.

Conclusion

The Samsung Galaxy S24 Ultra's camera system is designed to take amazing photos and videos. With its **200MP primary camera**, **zoom lenses**, **ultra-wide camera**, and **front camera**, you have all the tools you need to capture stunning images. The camera system also comes with a variety of tips and tricks to help you get the best shots, from using Night Mode for low-light photos to experimenting with Pro Mode for full control. Whether you're taking photos of people, landscapes, or objects, the Galaxy S24 Ultra ensures your pictures are always clear, sharp, and beautiful.

Chapter Five

Battery Life and Charging

The battery life and charging speed of a phone are important factors for many users. No one likes to run out of battery halfway through the day, and it's great when a phone charges quickly. In this chapter, we will explore everything you need to know about the **battery capacity**, **performance**, and the **charging options** available on the Samsung Galaxy S24 Ultra. We will also give you some useful tips on how to make the most of your battery.

5.1 Battery Capacity and Performance

The **battery** in the Samsung Galaxy S24 Ultra is an important feature because it powers the phone for everything you do on it. Whether you are playing games, watching videos, or browsing the web, the battery needs to last the entire day. Samsung has equipped the Galaxy S24 Ultra with a **5000mAh battery**.

What is 5000mAh?

- **5000mAh** (milliampere-hour) refers to the size of the battery. A bigger number means a larger battery that can last longer. The 5000mAh battery in the Galaxy S24 Ultra is quite large compared to many other phones, which often have smaller batteries, like 4000mAh or 3500mAh. A larger battery means that you can use your phone for a longer period before it needs to be charged again.

How does the battery perform?

- The **5000mAh battery** in the Galaxy S24 Ultra is designed to last a full day with normal usage. This means that if you are using your phone for things like browsing the internet, checking social media, or watching videos, you should have enough power to last from morning to night without worrying about charging it during the day.

- **Heavy Usage**: If you are someone who plays a lot of games, watches high-definition videos, or uses the phone for work and personal tasks, the 5000mAh battery should still perform well. The phone's energy-efficient processor, the **Snapdragon 8 Gen 3**, helps conserve power and prevent the battery from draining too quickly.

- **Light Usage**: If you mostly use your phone for texting, making calls, and browsing the web, the battery will last even longer. In fact, on light usage days, the battery could last even into the next day before needing a recharge.

In general, the **5000mAh battery** in the Galaxy S24 Ultra is more than enough for daily use. Samsung has designed this battery to handle different types of phone activities while making sure it lasts long enough to get you through the day.

5.2 Fast Charging and Wireless Charging

Charging your phone quickly is a big advantage, especially when you're in a rush or need to quickly top up your battery. The **Samsung Galaxy S24 Ultra** offers both **fast charging** and **wireless charging**, which are great features that make it easy to keep your phone powered up.

Fast Charging

- **What is Fast Charging?** Fast charging means that the phone can charge up much faster than regular charging. The Samsung Galaxy S24 Ultra supports **45W fast charging**. This means that the phone can charge up to 50% in about **30 minutes** with the right charger.

  If you need to charge your phone quickly, using a **45W fast charger** is the best option. You can easily get enough power for several hours of use in just a short amount of time, making it perfect for those moments when you are in a rush.

- **How does it work?** The Galaxy S24 Ultra uses a USB Type-C to Type-C charging cable, which is used for fast charging. This is a fast, efficient way to charge your phone, and it is much quicker than older charging methods. The 45W charging speed is only possible when you use a compatible charger, so make sure to use the right charger to get the fast charging benefits.

- **Real-Life Charging Times** In real-life situations, using the fast charger with the **Galaxy S24 Ultra**, you can expect your phone to go from 0% to 50% in around 30 minutes.

From 0% to full charge (100%), it will take about 1 hour to 1 hour and 30 minutes, depending on the usage and temperature of the phone. This is much faster than older phones that could take several hours to fully charge.

Wireless Charging

- **What is Wireless Charging?** Wireless charging is a convenient way to charge your phone without needing to plug in any cables. The **Galaxy S24 Ultra** supports **15W wireless charging**, which is a decent speed for wireless charging.

   To use wireless charging, all you need to do is place your phone on a wireless charging pad. There is no need to plug in any cables, making it easy to charge your phone when you're at home, at the office, or in a car that has wireless charging.

- **How does it work?** To use wireless charging, you need to place the phone on a **Qi-enabled wireless charging pad**. The charging pad uses electromagnetic fields to transfer power to the phone's battery, and it's a simple process that requires no physical connection between the charger and the phone.

- **What are the advantages of wireless charging?** Wireless charging is very convenient because it eliminates the need to mess around with cables. It is especially useful when you're charging your phone at your desk or at home, as you can simply place the phone on the charger without worrying about plugging it in.

- **The downside of wireless charging** The downside to wireless charging is that it's generally slower than wired charging. **15W wireless charging** is good, but it will still take longer to fully charge your phone compared to **45W wired charging**. However, the advantage of not needing to plug in cables makes it an attractive option for many users.

Reverse Wireless Charging

- Another useful feature of the Samsung Galaxy S24 Ultra is **reverse wireless charging**. This allows you to charge other devices, like wireless earbuds or a friend's phone, by placing them on the back of your Galaxy S24 Ultra. This is very useful in situations where you need to charge a small device but don't have access to a charger or power bank.

5.3 Battery Management Tips

While the Galaxy S24 Ultra comes with a large battery that performs well, it's always a good idea to make the most of your phone's battery life. Here are some helpful **battery management tips** to make sure you can use your phone all day without worrying about running out of power.

1. Adjust Screen Brightness

The screen is one of the main things that uses a lot of power on your phone. If the screen brightness is set too high, it can drain the battery quickly. You can save battery by adjusting the brightness to a lower level or turning on **adaptive brightness**, which automatically adjusts the screen's brightness based on your surroundings.

2. Use Power Saving Mode

The **Galaxy S24 Ultra** has a **power saving mode** that helps extend battery life. When you turn on power saving mode, the phone reduces the amount of energy it uses by limiting background activities, reducing screen brightness, and turning off some features. This is especially useful when your battery is getting low and you need it to last until you can charge it again.

3. Turn Off Unused Features

If you're not using features like Bluetooth, Wi-Fi, or location services, it's a good idea to turn them off. These features use power even when they're not actively being used, so turning them off can help save battery. You can always turn them back on when you need them.

4. Limit Background Apps

Many apps continue running in the background even when you're not using them. These apps can drain your battery without you even realizing it. You can go into the settings and close any unused apps to stop them from using up your battery. Another option is to use **Battery Optimization** in the settings to make sure apps don't consume too much battery when they're running in the background.

5. Use Dark Mode

The Galaxy S24 Ultra's screen uses **AMOLED technology**, which allows the screen to turn off individual pixels when displaying dark colors. By using **Dark Mode**, the phone will use less power because dark colors take up less energy on AMOLED screens. This is a simple way to save battery throughout the day.

6. Keep the Software Updated

Samsung regularly releases software updates to improve the phone's performance and battery life. Keeping your phone's software updated ensures that you're getting the latest improvements and fixes. Software updates can help optimize battery usage and fix any bugs that might be draining your battery.

7. Monitor Battery Usage

The Galaxy S24 Ultra has a feature that lets you see which apps are using the most battery. This is a great tool to identify apps that might be draining your battery and taking up too much power. You can check the **battery usage** in the settings and take action if you notice any app using more power than it should.

8. Avoid Extreme Temperatures

Extreme temperatures can affect your battery's performance. Try to avoid using your phone in places that are too hot or too cold. If your phone gets too hot, the battery will drain faster, and if it gets too cold, the battery may not work as well. Keep your phone at room temperature for the best performance.

Conclusion

The **battery life and charging** features of the Samsung Galaxy S24 Ultra make it a reliable device for daily use. With its large **5000mAh battery**, you can enjoy all your favorite apps and activities without worrying about running out of power. The **45W fast charging** ensures that your phone gets charged quickly, and the **15W wireless charging** offers convenience without the need for wires.

By following the **battery management tips** outlined in this chapter, you can get the most out of your phone's battery life. Whether you need to charge quickly, save battery when you're running low, or simply extend your phone's battery life, the Galaxy S24 Ultra has the tools to help you.

Chapter Six

S Pen and Productivity Features

In this chapter, we will explore the **S Pen** that comes with the Samsung Galaxy S24 Ultra. The S Pen is a special feature that allows you to do many things on your phone, like taking notes, drawing, and using productivity tools. It is not just a stylus; it's an important tool that can help you be more efficient and creative with your phone. Whether you are using it for work, school, or personal tasks, the S Pen makes your phone more versatile and powerful. We will go over the features of the S Pen, how to use it for note-taking and drawing, and some of the productivity tools it has to offer.

6.1 S Pen Overview and Features

The **S Pen** is a special stylus that comes with the **Samsung Galaxy S24 Ultra**. It's designed to let you interact with your phone in a more precise way, just like a pen on paper. Instead of using your finger to tap or swipe on the screen, you can use the S Pen to write, draw, and navigate with more accuracy.

The S Pen is built to work seamlessly with the phone's screen, making it feel natural to use. It attaches to the back of the phone, so you always have it with you, ready for use. The S Pen is **small and lightweight**, so it's easy to carry around, but it has a lot of powerful features that make it a valuable tool for anyone who wants to do more with their phone.

One of the key features of the S Pen is that it has **Bluetooth capabilities**. This means that you can use the S Pen to perform actions even when it's not directly touching the screen. For example, you can use it to control your music, take photos, or change slides in a presentation without even having to touch the phone. This makes it very convenient for presentations or when you want to control your phone from a distance.

Another important feature of the S Pen is its **pressure sensitivity**. This means that the harder you press with the pen, the thicker the lines will be when you write or draw. This makes it feel more like using a real pen or pencil, and it gives you more control over your creations.

The S Pen also has a **low latency** (delay), meaning there is almost no lag between when you use the pen and when it shows up on the screen. This makes writing and drawing feel very smooth and natural. Whether you are taking notes or drawing a picture, the S Pen responds quickly and accurately to your movements.

Overall, the S Pen is a great addition to the Samsung Galaxy S24 Ultra, making the phone easier to use for creative tasks, as well as for everyday activities like note-taking and navigating your phone's interface.

6.2 Note-Taking and Drawing Capabilities

One of the most popular uses for the **S Pen** is **note-taking**. Whether you are in a meeting, class, or just jotting down ideas, the S Pen helps you write and organize your notes quickly and easily. You don't need to open an app to start writing — just take out the S Pen, and you can begin writing directly on the screen.

Note-Taking Features

With the **S Pen**, you can take notes in a variety of ways:

- **Screen Off Memo**: One of the most useful features of the S Pen is **Screen Off Memo**. This allows you to start writing on the screen without having to unlock the phone or open any apps. You simply take the S Pen out of its slot, and you can begin writing on the screen instantly. This is perfect for quickly jotting down ideas, reminders, or notes when you don't have time to open a full note-taking app.

- **Note App**: If you need more space or want to organize your notes, the Samsung **Notes app** is a great tool for writing and organizing your notes. With the S Pen, you can easily create and organize different notes, add lists, or highlight important information. You can also draw diagrams or illustrations in your notes if that's helpful.

- **Handwriting to Text**: One cool feature of the S Pen is the ability to **convert your handwriting into text**. This is perfect if you prefer to write by hand but want your notes to be in typed form. After writing, you can use the **convert to text** feature, and it will turn your handwritten notes into typed text that you can edit and share.

- **Sticky Notes**: The S Pen allows you to create **sticky notes** on your screen. These are little notes that stay on your home screen as reminders, and you can easily edit or remove them. This is great for quick to-do lists or important tasks you need to keep track of throughout the day.

Drawing with the S Pen

The S Pen is also great for **drawing**. Whether you are an artist, designer, or just like to doodle, the S Pen provides a smooth and precise experience. With its **pressure sensitivity**, you can create light or heavy strokes, making it perfect for sketching or shading.

- **Drawing Apps**: There are several apps available for drawing, such as **Adobe Photoshop Sketch** and **Autodesk SketchBook**, which are compatible with the S Pen. These apps give you many different brushes and tools to help you create detailed artwork.
- **Artistic Control**: With the pressure sensitivity and the smooth response of the S Pen, you can control how thick or thin your lines are, just like you would with a real pencil or pen. This gives you a great deal of **artistic freedom** to create the designs you want.
- **Coloring**: The S Pen also works well for coloring. Many apps allow you to color in pictures, and the pen gives you more control over the coloring process than your finger

would. The small tip of the S Pen allows you to color within the lines and make fine details.

- **Digital Handwriting**: For people who like to handwrite their notes or thoughts but prefer to do it digitally, the S Pen is a great tool. You can write naturally and have it instantly saved as digital text, which is easy to store, search, and share.

6.3 Productivity Tools and Integrations

The S Pen isn't just for taking notes or drawing — it also has many **productivity tools** that can help you get more done. These tools help you use your phone in smarter, more efficient ways, whether for work, school, or personal tasks.

1. Air Actions

One of the standout productivity features of the S Pen is **Air Actions**. With Air Actions, the S Pen can control your phone by simply **gesturing** with it. You can move the S Pen in the air to perform certain actions, such as:

- **Changing Slides**: If you are giving a presentation and want to change slides, you can use the S Pen to flip through them by just moving the pen in the air.

- **Taking Photos**: You can use the S Pen as a remote shutter button for your camera. Just press the button on the S Pen to take a picture without having to touch the screen.
- **Controlling Media**: If you're listening to music or watching a video, you can use Air Actions to play, pause, skip, or rewind tracks and videos. This is especially useful when you don't want to touch your phone but still need to control it.

These features help you interact with your phone without needing to physically touch the screen, which is very convenient in many situations.

2. Samsung DeX

Another great tool for productivity is **Samsung DeX**. This feature allows you to connect your phone to a larger screen, such as a computer monitor or TV, and use it like a desktop computer. You can open multiple windows, drag and drop files, and use your phone just like you would a computer.

- **Using the S Pen with DeX**: When using Samsung DeX, you can use the S Pen to interact with the desktop interface. This makes it easy to navigate, write notes, or even draw directly on the screen. The S Pen makes working in a desktop-like environment more efficient, as it gives you precise control over what you're doing.

3. Multitasking

The Samsung Galaxy S24 Ultra is designed for **multitasking**, and the S Pen enhances that experience. With the S Pen, you can easily split the screen to view two apps at once. For example, you could have your email open on one side of the screen and a note-taking app on the other side, and you can quickly move between them without losing your place.

The S Pen also allows you to easily **drag and drop** items between apps. For example, you can copy text from a webpage and paste it into a document by simply using the S Pen to select, drag, and drop the text.

4. Translate and Screen Write

The S Pen can also be used for **translating text** or **annotating** images:

- **Translate**: You can use the S Pen to select text in a foreign language, and the phone will translate it for you in real-time. This is helpful for reading foreign websites or documents.
- **Screen Write**: If you want to annotate an image or webpage, you can use the S Pen to **write directly on the screen**. You can take a screenshot, and then immediately write or draw on it. This is great for leaving notes or making corrections.

5. Syncing with Microsoft Office

For those who need to use Microsoft Office apps like Word, Excel, and PowerPoint, the S Pen works well with these apps. You can write, edit, and navigate through documents with precision. The integration with **OneDrive** also allows you to easily sync your documents across different devices, so you can continue working from anywhere.

Conclusion

The **S Pen** on the Samsung Galaxy S24 Ultra is more than just a stylus; it's a powerful tool that can help you be more productive and creative. Whether you are **taking notes**, **drawing**, or using the **productivity**

tools, the S Pen gives you precise control over your phone. With features like **Air Actions**, **Samsung DeX**, and **Screen Write**, you can do more with your phone, making it a great tool for work, school, and personal tasks. The **S Pen** truly makes the **Samsung Galaxy S24 Ultra** an all-in-one device that can meet many of your needs, whether you're using it for everyday activities or more complex tasks.

Chapter Seven

Display and Audio

In this chapter, we will take a close look at the **display** and **audio** features of the Samsung Galaxy S24 Ultra. These two elements are key to ensuring you enjoy the full experience of using the phone. Whether you are watching videos, playing games, browsing photos, or listening to music, the **display** and **audio** quality play a huge part in how enjoyable and immersive your phone experience will be. Let's explore how the Samsung Galaxy S24 Ultra brings together an impressive display and strong audio performance for an all-around better user experience.

7.1 Adaptive 120Hz Refresh Rate

One of the standout features of the Samsung Galaxy S24 Ultra's display is its **Adaptive 120Hz Refresh Rate**. But what exactly does that mean? To understand this better, let's first talk about what a **refresh rate** is.

What is a Refresh Rate?

The refresh rate refers to how many times per second the screen updates the image you see. It's measured in **Hertz (Hz)**. If you have a screen with a **60Hz refresh rate**, the image refreshes 60 times per second. Higher refresh rates mean that the screen updates more often, making the display feel smoother and more responsive.

For example, when you scroll through a webpage, a higher refresh rate makes the text and images appear to move more smoothly. The more times the screen refreshes, the less likely you are to see any blurriness or choppiness when you're moving things on the screen. So, a **higher refresh rate** improves the **smoothness** of everything you do on your phone.

120Hz Adaptive Refresh Rate

The Samsung Galaxy S24 Ultra takes this even further with an **Adaptive 120Hz Refresh Rate**. This means that the refresh rate can change depending on what you are doing on the phone. For example, if you are watching a video or playing a game, the phone will increase the refresh rate to **120Hz for a smoother experience**. But, when you're reading a static page or using an app that doesn't require a fast refresh rate, it will automatically reduce the refresh rate to **60Hz** or even **1Hz** in some cases.

This **adaptive** refresh rate helps to **save battery** because the phone doesn't have to refresh the screen 120 times per second all the time. It only does it when needed, which means the battery lasts longer.

How Does This Affect Your Experience?

When you use the Samsung Galaxy S24 Ultra, you'll notice that scrolling through apps, webpages, and social media feels much smoother compared to phones with lower refresh rates. It's especially noticeable when you're playing games or watching videos. A 120Hz refresh rate makes games and videos look **sharper**, **faster**, and more **fluid**, making everything feel more real and immersive.

With the **Adaptive 120Hz Refresh Rate**, you get the best of both worlds: a smooth display when you need it, and battery savings when you don't. It's an intelligent system that makes using the phone both enjoyable and efficient.

7.2 HDR10+ and Display Quality

Another key feature of the Samsung Galaxy S24 Ultra's display is its support for **HDR10+**. To understand this feature, let's first talk about **what HDR means**.

What is HDR?

HDR stands for **High Dynamic Range**. It's a technology used in displays to enhance the **brightness**, **contrast**, and **color** of what you see on the screen. With HDR, images appear more **lifelike**, with deeper blacks, brighter whites, and more vibrant colors.

When watching movies or videos on a screen that supports HDR, the picture quality is much more detailed. Shadows and bright areas in the image look better, and colors are richer. **HDR10+** is an even better version of HDR that adapts the display settings for each scene of a video, providing **dynamic** adjustments to the picture quality.

HDR10+ in the Galaxy S24 Ultra

The **Samsung Galaxy S24 Ultra** supports **HDR10+**, meaning that it can display **content** with **greater contrast** and **vivid colors**. When you're watching a movie or video that is filmed in HDR10+ (many modern movies and shows support this format), you'll see much better picture quality compared to standard displays. This is because the display on the

Galaxy S24 Ultra can adjust the brightness and contrast for each scene to make sure it looks perfect.

For example, in a movie with both very dark and very bright scenes, HDR10+ makes sure the details in the shadows are visible while the bright areas do not lose their detail. It creates a more balanced and visually pleasing experience. Colors will pop and be more accurate, making the picture appear richer and more vibrant.

How Does HDR10+ Improve Viewing?

When watching HDR10+ content on the Samsung Galaxy S24 Ultra, you'll notice that the picture looks **brighter**, **more colorful**, and more **detailed**. Dark scenes will have more visible details, and bright scenes will appear clearer. Whether you are watching a movie, playing a game, or viewing photos, the HDR10+ technology makes everything look more **realistic** and **immersive**.

This technology is great for anyone who enjoys watching videos or movies on their phone. With HDR10+ support, the Galaxy S24 Ultra's display brings out the best in **content**, making it look **incredible** on the phone's large and vibrant screen.

7.3 Audio Performance and Speakers

While the display quality is important, the **audio performance** of the Samsung Galaxy S24 Ultra is just as crucial for a full multimedia experience. Whether you are watching videos, listening to music, or making calls, the quality of the sound you hear on your phone can make a big difference in how much you enjoy using it.

Stereo Speakers by AKG

The **Samsung Galaxy S24 Ultra** comes with **stereo speakers** that are tuned by **AKG**, a brand known for producing high-quality audio equipment. Stereo speakers mean that there are two speakers in the phone — one at the bottom and one at the top — which work together to create a more **immersive sound experience**. This setup creates sound that feels like it is coming from multiple directions, making the listening experience more dynamic.

The **AKG tuning** helps to deliver clearer, more balanced sound with deep bass, crisp treble, and clear mid-tones. Whether you are listening to music, watching a movie, or playing a game, the sound will be clear and enjoyable.

Dolby Atmos Support

To make the audio even better, the Samsung Galaxy S24 Ultra supports **Dolby Atmos**, a surround sound technology that enhances the audio experience by making the sound feel more three-dimensional. Dolby Atmos creates a more immersive environment by simulating the feeling that sound is coming from all around you — even from above and below.

When you listen to music or watch videos with Dolby Atmos, you will notice that the audio feels richer and fuller. The **soundstage** (the space in which you hear sound) feels wider and more expansive, making it easier to feel as if you're surrounded by sound. This is particularly noticeable in action scenes of movies or in games where you want to hear every detail of the soundscape.

Volume and Clarity

The stereo speakers and Dolby Atmos support on the Galaxy S24 Ultra also ensure that the **volume** is loud enough for most situations. Whether you are watching videos on a crowded bus, playing a game at home, or listening to music in the park, the speakers will provide enough volume for you to hear everything clearly. The sound quality is not only loud but also clear, with minimal distortion even at higher volumes.

If you enjoy listening to **music**, **podcasts**, or **audiobooks**, you'll appreciate the clear and rich sound of the Galaxy S24 Ultra. The stereo speakers and Dolby Atmos work together to give you a great listening experience, making it easier to enjoy audio content without the need for headphones.

Headphone and Bluetooth Audio Support

While the built-in speakers are excellent, the Galaxy S24 Ultra also supports **Bluetooth audio**. If you prefer listening with **wireless headphones** or a **Bluetooth speaker**, the phone can connect seamlessly with these devices. The audio quality over Bluetooth is high, and you can enjoy **lossless audio** when paired with compatible devices.

For those who prefer wired headphones, the phone also has a **USB-C port**, which can be used to connect headphones directly for high-quality sound.

Conclusion

The **display** and **audio** of the Samsung Galaxy S24 Ultra work together to create a complete and immersive experience for users. The **Adaptive 120Hz Refresh Rate** provides a smooth and responsive display, making everything from scrolling to gaming feel fluid and fast. The **HDR10+ support** enhances your viewing experience by providing better contrast, brightness, and color, so videos and images look richer and more realistic.

In terms of audio, the **stereo speakers** tuned by **AKG** deliver clear and powerful sound, while **Dolby Atmos** adds a surround-sound effect that makes movies, music, and games more immersive. The sound is loud, clear, and full of detail, making it a pleasure to listen to audio content, whether through the built-in speakers or Bluetooth-connected devices.

All of these features combined make the Samsung Galaxy S24 Ultra an excellent phone for anyone who values great display and audio quality. Whether you are watching videos, playing games, or listening to music, the S24 Ultra provides a top-tier experience that brings your content to life.

Chapter Eight

Connectivity and 5G

In today's world, we use our phones for much more than just calling and texting. We rely on them for internet browsing, streaming videos, gaming, and connecting with others around the world. This means that a phone's **connectivity** features—how it connects to the internet, networks, and other devices—are more important than ever. The Samsung Galaxy S24 Ultra is packed with advanced features to keep you connected wherever you go. This chapter will explore the **5G support**, **Wi-Fi**, **Bluetooth**, **NFC**, and **Dual SIM** features of the Galaxy S24 Ultra to help you understand how this phone keeps you connected in all situations.

8.1 5G Support and Performance

5G is the **fifth generation of mobile networks**. It's the latest technology for connecting to the internet through your phone, and it offers **faster speeds**, **better reliability**, and **lower latency** (the time it takes for data to travel from one place to another). The

Samsung Galaxy S24 Ultra supports **5G**, which means you can take advantage of all these benefits.

What Does 5G Mean for You?

Before 5G, we had **4G LTE**, which was already fast enough for most activities like browsing the web, streaming music, and video chatting. However, 5G is **significantly faster** than 4G. With 5G, you can download movies, upload photos, and stream high-quality videos in **seconds**. It's like upgrading from a regular highway to a super-fast, high-speed train.

5G is designed to handle much more data at once. This means that even when many people are using the network at the same time, your connection will remain strong and fast. It's especially useful for activities like **streaming high-definition video**, **playing mobile games**, or using apps that need a lot of internet bandwidth.

The **Samsung Galaxy S24 Ultra** comes with **5G compatibility**, meaning it can connect to the latest 5G networks in your area. This makes the phone **future-proof**, so it will stay fast and efficient as 5G networks continue to expand and improve.

Performance of 5G on the Galaxy S24 Ultra

With **5G** support, the Galaxy S24 Ultra can download data and stream content at incredible speeds. For example, you could download an entire **HD movie** in just a few minutes or **upload high-resolution photos** almost instantly.

The **performance** of 5G can vary based on where you are, depending on whether you are in a 5G-covered area and how strong the 5G signal is. **Sub-6GHz 5G** is the more common form of 5G, providing broad coverage and decent speeds. However, **mmWave 5G**, a faster version of 5G, may be available in some locations, giving you **super-fast speeds** for data-hungry activities.

While you are on a **5G connection**, you can expect **low latency**, meaning that data will be transferred quickly. This is important for applications like **video calls**, **online gaming**, and **live streaming**, where small delays can make a big difference. The low latency also helps with real-time communication, like video conferencing or virtual reality, where timing is crucial.

In short, **5G support** on the Samsung Galaxy S24 Ultra makes sure that your phone can handle the internet demands of today and in the future. Whether you are downloading large files, streaming videos in high definition, or playing online games, 5G ensures you have the speed and performance to enjoy all of it without interruptions.

8.2 Wi-Fi, Bluetooth, and NFC

A phone's **connectivity** is not just about 5G; it also needs to connect to **Wi-Fi networks**, **Bluetooth devices**, and **NFC-enabled tools**. The Samsung Galaxy S24 Ultra offers top-notch performance in all of these areas.

Wi-Fi

Wi-Fi is the technology that allows your phone to connect to the internet using a wireless network, often in your home, office, or public spaces like coffee shops and airports. The Galaxy S24 Ultra supports **Wi-Fi 6** (also known as **802.11ax**), which is the latest version of Wi-Fi technology.

- **What is Wi-Fi 6?** Wi-Fi 6 offers several improvements over previous Wi-Fi versions. It provides faster speeds, better performance when many devices are connected at once, and improved battery life for your phone. This is especially useful in places with a lot of people using the internet at the same time, like offices, stadiums, or cafes.

With Wi-Fi 6, the Samsung Galaxy S24 Ultra can maintain strong and fast internet speeds, even when there are many devices connected to the same network. If you are streaming videos, working from home, or video calling with friends, Wi-Fi 6 helps ensure a smooth and fast connection.

Bluetooth

Bluetooth is another important technology for connecting your phone to other devices, like wireless headphones, speakers, fitness trackers, or your car. The **Samsung Galaxy S24 Ultra** supports **Bluetooth 5.3**, which is the latest version of Bluetooth.

- **What is Bluetooth 5.3?** Bluetooth 5.3 provides faster speeds, better range, and lower energy consumption than older versions of Bluetooth. This means you can connect to Bluetooth devices faster, enjoy a more stable connection, and use less battery while doing so. Whether you are listening to music through wireless headphones, connecting to a Bluetooth speaker, or using a Bluetooth fitness tracker, Bluetooth 5.3 ensures that these connections are quick and reliable.

- **Dual Audio**: Bluetooth 5.3 also allows you to stream audio to **two devices at the same time**. For example, you can connect your phone to both a Bluetooth speaker and a pair of Bluetooth headphones, so everyone can listen to the same music or movie without needing to share one device.

NFC (Near Field Communication)

NFC is a short-range wireless technology that allows devices to communicate with each other by simply being close to each other. The **Samsung Galaxy S24 Ultra** comes with **NFC support**, meaning it can connect to other NFC-enabled devices for tasks like making payments, exchanging files, or connecting to other devices.

- **What is NFC used for?**
  - **Mobile Payments**: One of the most popular uses for NFC is making **contactless payments**. With NFC, you can simply hold your Galaxy S24 Ultra

near a payment terminal, and the phone will automatically make the payment using **Samsung Pay** or another compatible mobile payment system. This is quick, secure, and easy.

- ○ **File Sharing**: NFC can also be used for quick file sharing between two devices. If you want to send a picture, contact information, or a website link, you can touch your phone to another NFC-enabled device, and the file will transfer instantly.
- ○ **Pairing Devices**: NFC is also used for quickly pairing your phone with devices like Bluetooth speakers or headphones. By tapping your phone near an NFC-enabled device, it will automatically pair, saving you the time of manually searching for and connecting to the device.

In summary, the Samsung Galaxy S24 Ultra offers all the latest connectivity features, from **Wi-Fi 6** for faster internet connections to **Bluetooth 5.3** for seamless connections with wireless devices. The **NFC** functionality makes it easy to make payments, share files, and pair devices with a simple tap.

8.3 Dual SIM and eSIM Features

The Samsung Galaxy S24 Ultra also comes with **Dual SIM** and **eSIM** capabilities. These features are great for people who want to use two phone numbers or data plans on the same device.

Dual SIM

A **Dual SIM** phone allows you to use two SIM cards in one device. This means you can have two phone numbers on the same phone, making it easier to separate work and personal calls or use different carriers for better coverage. Dual SIM functionality is especially useful for people who travel frequently or who want to manage different plans for data and calls.

The Samsung Galaxy S24 Ultra supports **Dual SIM**, meaning it can handle two physical SIM cards at once. This is ideal for people who want to keep two phone numbers active on the same device.

- **How Does Dual SIM Work?** With **Dual SIM**, you can make calls, send messages, and use data from either of the two SIM cards. You can easily switch between the two numbers in the phone's settings, and you can even customize which SIM to use for different purposes. For example, you could use one SIM for local calls and the other for international data, saving you money when traveling.

eSIM

In addition to Dual SIM, the Samsung Galaxy S24 Ultra also supports **eSIM**, which stands for **embedded SIM**. An eSIM is a digital SIM that is built into the phone, so you don't need a physical SIM card. Instead, you can download a mobile plan directly onto your phone from your carrier. This makes it easy to switch between carriers or plans without needing to swap physical SIM cards.

- **Benefits of eSIM**
  - **Convenience**: You don't need to worry about losing or damaging a physical SIM card. Everything is stored digitally on the phone.
  - **Easy to Switch**: Switching between carriers is easier because you can change plans without needing to visit a store or get a new SIM card.
  - **Great for Travelers**: eSIM is perfect for people who travel frequently. You can

easily add a local plan when you arrive in a new country, avoiding expensive roaming charges from your home carrier.

With both **Dual SIM** and **eSIM**, the Galaxy S24 Ultra offers flexible options for managing multiple phone numbers and data plans.

Conclusion

The Samsung Galaxy S24 Ultra is packed with advanced **connectivity** features to help you stay connected to the world around you. With **5G support**, you can experience lightning-fast internet speeds, making it easier to download, upload, and stream content. **Wi-Fi 6**, **Bluetooth 5.3**, and **NFC** provide fast, reliable connections to other devices, while **Dual SIM** and **eSIM** offer flexibility for managing multiple phone numbers and data plans.

These connectivity features make the Samsung Galaxy S24 Ultra an excellent choice for anyone who needs fast internet, reliable connections, and the ability to manage multiple phone numbers in one device. Whether you're working, traveling, or enjoying entertainment, the Galaxy S24 Ultra keeps you connected in every situation.

Chapter Nine

Tips and Tricks for Users

In this chapter, we will share some **tips and tricks** for getting the most out of your Samsung Galaxy S24 Ultra. The Galaxy S24 Ultra is a powerful phone with many features that you might not be aware of. Whether you want to learn about **hidden features**, improve your **battery life**, or get better at using the **camera**, we have tips and tricks to make your experience with this phone even better.

9.1 Hidden Features of the Galaxy S24 Ultra

The Samsung Galaxy S24 Ultra is packed with **useful features**, some of which may be hidden or not obvious at first glance. Let's explore a few of the **hidden features** you can find on this phone that can improve your overall experience.

1. Screen Off Memo

One of the coolest hidden features of the Galaxy S24 Ultra is **Screen Off Memo**. This feature allows you to write quick notes on the screen without even unlocking your phone. Here's how it works:

- Take out the **S Pen** from its slot.
- Even if the screen is off, the phone will detect the S Pen and let you write directly on the screen.
- You can jot down quick ideas, reminders, or notes, and when you're done, the phone will save them automatically in the **Notes** app. This feature is super useful when you need to capture an idea or remember something quickly.

2. Edge Panels

The **Edge Panels** feature lets you add quick access shortcuts to the side of your screen. Instead of searching for apps in your apps list, you can swipe from the edge of your screen to pull up your most-used apps or tools. To set up **Edge Panels**:

- Go to **Settings** > **Display** > **Edge Panels**.
- You can customize the panel to show apps, contacts, or tools like the calculator, weather, or screen recorder. This feature saves time and makes it easier to access your favorite apps.

3. One-Handed Mode

The Galaxy S24 Ultra has a large screen, which can sometimes make it difficult to use with just one hand. **One-Handed Mode** solves this problem by shrinking the screen so you can reach everything with one hand. To enable **One-Handed Mode**:

- Go to **Settings** > **Advanced Features** > **One-Handed Mode**.
- You can choose to use gestures or the home button to reduce the screen size. Now, you can use your phone more easily with just one hand, especially when you need to type or navigate through apps.

4. App Pair

App Pair lets you open two apps at the same time, side by side, with a single tap. For example, you can open your **email** and **calendar** at the same time, which is perfect for multitasking. To set up **App Pair**:

- Go to **Settings** > **Advanced Features** > **Multi-Window** > **App Pair**.
- Select the two apps you want to open together. Now, you can quickly launch two apps side by side without having to manually open each one.

5. Quick Screenshot and Editing

You can quickly take a screenshot by swiping the side of your hand across the screen. Once the screenshot is captured, you can immediately edit it by drawing, cropping, or adding text. To take a screenshot:

- Swipe the edge of your hand across the screen.
- After the screenshot is taken, tap **Edit** to make quick changes before saving it. This is a fast way to capture and edit important information.

6. Bixby Routines

Bixby Routines allow you to automate tasks on your phone. You can set up routines to make your phone do certain things at specific times, like turning on **Do Not Disturb** during meetings or turning off Wi-Fi when you leave home. To set up **Bixby Routines**:

- Go to **Settings** > **Advanced Features** > **Bixby Routines**.
- You can create custom routines for different situations, such as when you're driving, at work, or at home. Bixby Routines help automate your phone to make it work for you, saving you time and effort.

9.2 How to Maximize Battery Life

Battery life is one of the most important factors when using a smartphone. The Samsung Galaxy S24 Ultra comes with a large **5000mAh battery**, but with heavy usage, you might find the need to maximize battery life. Here are some tips on how to get the most out of your phone's battery.

1. Use Power Saving Mode

The Galaxy S24 Ultra has a **Power Saving Mode** that helps extend battery life. When this mode is turned on, the phone limits background processes, reduces screen brightness, and disables certain features to save energy. To activate **Power Saving Mode**:

- Go to **Settings** > **Battery and Device Care** > **Battery** > **Power Saving Mode**.
- Toggle it on, and you'll see options to adjust the settings. This is a great way to stretch out your battery during long days when you might not have access to a charger.

2. Use Adaptive Brightness

The screen is one of the biggest battery drainers on your phone. The Galaxy S24 Ultra comes with **Adaptive Brightness**, which automatically adjusts the screen brightness based on your environment. To enable **Adaptive Brightness**:

- Go to **Settings** > **Display** > **Adaptive Brightness**.
- Turn on the toggle to allow the phone to adjust the brightness for you. This helps save battery by reducing brightness in dark environments and increasing it when you're outside in bright light.

3. Turn Off Unnecessary Features

There are certain features on your phone that use battery power even when you're not using them. To conserve energy, turn off features like **Bluetooth**, **Wi-Fi**, and **Location Services** when you don't need them. To quickly turn off these features:

- Swipe down from the top of the screen to open the **Quick Settings Menu**.
- Toggle off **Bluetooth**, **Wi-Fi**, and **Location** if you're not using them.

4. Use Dark Mode

The Galaxy S24 Ultra has an **AMOLED display**, which means it can turn off individual pixels when displaying dark colors. By using **Dark Mode**, you save battery because dark pixels use less power. To enable **Dark Mode**:

- Go to **Settings** > **Display** > **Dark Mode**.
- Turn it on, and enjoy a battery-friendly, eye-friendly experience.

5. Limit Background Apps

Many apps continue to run in the background, using up battery power even when you're not actively using them. You can limit the number of background apps to save battery. To limit background apps:

- Go to **Settings** > **Battery and Device Care** > **Battery** > **Background Usage Limits**.
- Here, you can limit apps from running in the background when not in use.

6. Enable Battery Optimization

Battery optimization helps manage how apps use power. Some apps can use more power than necessary, so optimizing them will ensure they don't drain your battery. To enable **Battery Optimization**:

- Go to **Settings** > **Battery and Device Care** > **Battery** > **Battery Optimization**.
- You can choose which apps to optimize or let the phone optimize them automatically.

9.3 Camera Hacks and Settings

The camera is one of the main features of the Samsung Galaxy S24 Ultra, and it comes with a range of settings and tools to help you take stunning photos and videos. Let's explore some useful **camera hacks** and settings to get the best results.

1. Use Pro Mode for Better Control

If you want more control over your photos, try using **Pro Mode**. This mode lets you adjust settings like **ISO**, **shutter speed**, and **white balance**, giving you more creative control over your shots. To activate **Pro Mode**:

- Open the **Camera** app and swipe to the **More** tab.
- Select **Pro Mode**, and you'll see manual controls for each setting. Pro Mode is great for capturing high-quality images, especially in

difficult lighting conditions or when you want to experiment with different settings.

2. Take Better Low-Light Photos with Night Mode

Night Mode is designed to help you take clearer, brighter photos in low light. The camera will take several photos and combine them to create a brighter image with less noise. To use **Night Mode**:

- Open the **Camera** app and tap the **Night Mode** icon (it looks like a moon).
- Hold the phone steady while it takes the photo. Night Mode is great for capturing photos in dimly lit environments, such as indoors at night or outside in low light.

3. Use the 200MP Camera for Detailed Photos

The Samsung Galaxy S24 Ultra has a **200MP primary camera**, which allows you to capture extremely detailed photos. This is perfect for close-ups or when you want to zoom in on an image without losing clarity. To use the **200MP camera**:

- Open the **Camera** app and switch to **Pro Mode**.
- Select the **200MP option**. This setting is perfect when you need maximum detail, like

capturing nature scenes or photographing intricate objects.

4. Take Portrait Mode Shots for Stunning Photos

Portrait Mode lets you take professional-looking photos with a blurred background (also known as **bokeh** effect). This helps your subject stand out, whether it's a person, pet, or object. To use **Portrait Mode**:

- Open the **Camera** app and swipe to **Portrait Mode**.
- Focus on your subject and snap the picture. Portrait Mode works best in good lighting, so try to use it in bright areas to get the best effect.

5. Use the Zoom Lenses for Distant Subjects

The Samsung Galaxy S24 Ultra comes with a **telephoto lens** and a **periscope lens**, allowing you to zoom in on distant subjects without losing image quality. To use **zoom**:

- Open the **Camera** app and pinch the screen to zoom in.
- You can use the **telephoto lens** for **3x zoom** or the **periscope lens** for **10x zoom**. These lenses

help you capture detailed shots from far away, such as wildlife, landscapes, or events.

6. Enable Super Steady Mode for Smooth Videos

If you like to record videos, **Super Steady Mode** is a great feature to ensure your footage is smooth and stable, even if you're moving around. To enable **Super Steady Mode**:

- Open the **Camera** app and switch to **Video Mode**.
- Tap the **Super Steady** icon. This mode is perfect for action shots, such as when you're walking, running, or filming while on the move.

Conclusion

The **Samsung Galaxy S24 Ultra** is packed with features that help you get the most out of your phone. From **hidden features** like **Screen Off Memo** and **Edge Panels** to tips for **maximizing battery life** and **camera hacks**, there's a lot to explore. By using these tips and tricks, you can enhance your experience with the phone and make it work even better for your needs. Whether you're looking to capture perfect photos, extend your battery life, or just make your phone more efficient, the Galaxy S24 Ultra has everything you need to do so.

Chapter Ten

Accessories and Add-ons

In this chapter, we will explore some of the **accessories** and **add-ons** that can help you get the most out of your **Samsung Galaxy S24 Ultra**. The phone itself is a powerful and feature-rich device, but there are many **official accessories** and useful add-ons that can enhance its performance, protect it, and make your daily use more convenient. We will take a look at the **official Samsung accessories**, the best **cases and screen protectors**, and the importance of **wireless chargers** and other gear that can make your experience even better.

10.1 Official Samsung Accessories

Samsung offers a variety of **official accessories** specifically designed for the Galaxy S24 Ultra. These accessories are made to work seamlessly with your phone, ensuring the best possible performance and compatibility. Here are some of the best official accessories you can use with your Samsung Galaxy S24 Ultra:

1. Samsung S Pen

The **S Pen** is one of the standout features of the Galaxy S24 Ultra. While the phone comes with the S Pen included, there are also **official Samsung accessories** that improve its functionality. The **S Pen** allows you to write, draw, and control your phone with greater precision.

Some **S Pen-related accessories** include:

- **S Pen Case**: A special case that holds your S Pen in place when it's not in use, so you don't have to worry about losing it. This case keeps the S Pen securely attached to the phone.
- **Replacement S Pens**: If your S Pen gets damaged or lost, Samsung offers official replacement pens that work just as well as the original one.

The S Pen enhances your productivity and creativity, allowing you to take quick notes, draw, or control your phone with a simple gesture.

2. Samsung Galaxy Buds

The **Samsung Galaxy Buds** are wireless earbuds designed for the Galaxy S24 Ultra. If you enjoy listening to music or making calls, these buds offer great sound quality, comfort, and connectivity.

Key features include:

- **Clear sound**: The Galaxy Buds provide crisp and clear audio, making them perfect for listening to music, podcasts, or taking calls.
- **Noise cancellation**: Some versions of the Galaxy Buds include active noise cancellation (ANC), helping to block out background noise for better sound quality, especially in noisy environments.
- **Wireless charging**: These earbuds charge wirelessly using a **Qi-compatible charger**, which is convenient and easy to use.

Samsung offers different versions of the **Galaxy Buds**, such as the **Galaxy Buds Pro**, **Galaxy Buds Live**, and **Galaxy Buds2**, each offering varying levels of sound quality, comfort, and features like water resistance or noise cancellation.

3. Samsung Smartwatch

The **Samsung Galaxy Watch** is an excellent companion for your Galaxy S24 Ultra. It helps you stay connected, track your health, and manage your notifications without needing to check your phone.

Key features of the **Galaxy Watch** include:

- **Fitness tracking**: The Galaxy Watch can track your heart rate, steps, sleep, and more. It's a great tool for anyone who wants to stay on top of their health and fitness goals.
- **Notifications**: You can receive notifications directly on your wrist, so you never miss a call, text, or app alert.
- **Samsung Pay**: With the Galaxy Watch, you can make payments right from your wrist using Samsung Pay, without needing to pull out your phone.

Whether you want to track your workouts, stay connected on the go, or manage your notifications hands-free, the **Samsung Galaxy Watch** is a perfect accessory for the Galaxy S24 Ultra.

4. Samsung Wireless Charger

If you want to charge your Galaxy S24 Ultra without plugging in cables, the **Samsung Wireless Charger** is the perfect accessory. Samsung offers a variety of **wireless charging pads and stands**, making it easy to charge your phone quickly and wirelessly.

Key features of the **Samsung Wireless Charger** include:

- **Fast charging**: Samsung's wireless chargers support fast charging, so you can quickly charge your phone without the hassle of plugging in cables.
- **Convenience**: Simply place your phone on the charger, and it will begin charging instantly. Some wireless chargers also have the ability to charge other devices, like your Galaxy Buds or smartwatch, at the same time.

A **wireless charger** offers the convenience of cable-free charging, keeping your charging area neat and organized while providing fast and efficient charging.

10.2 Best Cases and Screen Protectors

Protecting your phone is important to ensure it lasts for as long as possible. The **Samsung Galaxy S24 Ultra** is a premium device with a large display and sleek design, so it's a good idea to use **cases and screen protectors** to keep it safe from scratches, drops, and other potential damage.

Here are some of the best options to protect your Galaxy S24 Ultra:

1. Samsung Official Cases

Samsung offers a variety of **official cases** for the Galaxy S24 Ultra, each designed to offer different types of protection while maintaining the phone's sleek look. Here are some popular options:

- **Samsung Silicone Cover**: The **Silicone Cover** is soft to the touch and provides a comfortable grip while offering good protection from drops and scratches. It's slim, lightweight, and available in various colors to match your style.
- **Samsung Clear View Cover**: The **Clear View Cover** lets you see your phone's notifications and time through the front cover without opening the case. It offers protection for both the front and back of your phone while still allowing you to interact with your phone's screen.
- **Samsung Leather Cover**: For a more premium feel, the **Leather Cover** offers a luxurious, soft leather texture that feels great in your hand. It provides excellent protection and adds a touch of elegance to your phone.
- **Samsung Rugged Protective Case**: If you're someone who tends to drop your phone or use it in rough conditions, the **Rugged Protective Case** offers extra protection. This case is made

from durable materials and can handle drops, bumps, and scratches, making it a good choice for active users.

These official Samsung cases are designed to fit the Galaxy S24 Ultra perfectly and provide reliable protection against everyday wear and tear.

2. Third-Party Cases

In addition to Samsung's official cases, there are also many high-quality **third-party cases** available for the Galaxy S24 Ultra. Some of the most popular third-party brands include:

- **OtterBox**: Known for making heavy-duty phone cases, **OtterBox** offers excellent protection for people who want their phones to survive tough conditions. They offer different types of cases, including slim cases and more rugged options.
- **Spigen**: **Spigen** offers a wide range of stylish and protective cases for the Galaxy S24 Ultra, including slim cases and cases with built-in stands for hands-free viewing.
- **UAG (Urban Armor Gear)**: UAG cases are built to withstand drops and rough handling. They're known for their durability and military-grade protection, making them

perfect for anyone who needs extra protection.

No matter your preference, you can find a case that suits your needs, whether you're looking for something stylish, slim, rugged, or with added features.

3. Screen Protectors

In addition to cases, **screen protectors** are a must-have accessory to keep your phone's display safe from scratches, smudges, and cracks. The **Galaxy S24 Ultra** has a large, high-quality screen that can easily get scratched if not properly protected.

There are two main types of screen protectors you can choose from:

- **Tempered Glass Screen Protectors**: **Tempered glass** provides the best protection against scratches and impacts. It is thicker and more durable than plastic screen protectors and offers a smooth touch experience. **Tempered glass** also maintains the clarity and brightness of the screen, ensuring that your display looks as good as it did before.
- **Plastic Film Screen Protectors**: **Plastic film** protectors are thinner and more flexible, but

they don't offer the same level of protection as tempered glass. They can protect against minor scratches but are not as effective at preventing cracks from drops.

Samsung offers official **screen protectors** for the Galaxy S24 Ultra, and there are also plenty of high-quality third-party options to choose from.

10.3 Wireless Chargers and Other Gear

In addition to cases, screen protectors, and the S Pen, there are a number of **other accessories and gear** that can enhance your experience with the Samsung Galaxy S24 Ultra. These accessories make using your phone more convenient, improve its functionality, and help you stay connected.

1. Wireless Chargers

Wireless chargers are a must-have accessory for anyone who wants the convenience of charging their phone without dealing with tangled cables. The **Samsung Galaxy S24 Ultra** supports **wireless charging**, and Samsung offers a variety of **wireless charging pads and stands**.

Some options include:

- **Samsung Wireless Charger Pad**: This is a sleek, compact charging pad that allows you to place your phone on top and start charging without plugging in any cables. It supports fast charging and is perfect for charging your phone at home or in the office.
- **Samsung Wireless Charging Stand**: This stand allows you to place your phone in an upright position while it charges. It's perfect for watching videos, browsing, or using your phone while it charges. The **Charging Stand** also supports fast charging.

Wireless chargers are great because they eliminate the need for messy cables and allow for convenient charging.

2. Power Banks and Portable Chargers

If you're always on the go, a **power bank** or **portable charger** can be a lifesaver. These portable devices allow you to charge your **Galaxy S24 Ultra** when you're away from an outlet.

- **Samsung Portable Battery Pack**: Samsung offers its own range of **portable chargers**, which are compact and efficient. You can take them with you wherever you go, ensuring that your phone stays charged throughout the day.

- **Third-Party Power Banks**: Brands like **Anker**, **RAVPower**, and **Aukey** offer high-quality power banks that can charge your phone multiple times on a single charge. Many of these power banks support **fast charging**, so your phone will be ready to go in no time.

A **power bank** is an essential accessory for anyone who needs to charge their phone while traveling, commuting, or away from home.

Conclusion

The **Samsung Galaxy S24 Ultra** is a powerful smartphone, but it can be even better with the right accessories. Whether you need **protection** for your phone with a **case and screen protector**, **enhanced productivity** with the **S Pen**, or the convenience of **wireless charging**, Samsung offers many official accessories that can improve your phone experience. Additionally, there are many **third-party accessories** available that provide extra features, protection, and convenience. By adding the right accessories to your

Galaxy S24 Ultra, you can make your phone even more useful and enjoyable to use.

Chapter Eleven

Troubleshooting and FAQs

The **Samsung Galaxy S24 Ultra** is a highly advanced phone, but like any technology, you may run into some problems from time to time. In this chapter, we'll cover some **common issues** that users face with the Galaxy S24 Ultra, and we'll provide **solutions** to fix them. We'll also explain how to perform a **factory reset** and **backup** your phone to protect your data. Finally, we'll answer some of the **frequently asked questions (FAQs)** to help you understand how to use the phone more effectively.

11.1 Common Issues and Solutions

While the Galaxy S24 Ultra is a powerful phone, you might experience some problems during normal use. Here are some of the most common issues users face and their solutions.

1. Battery Draining Too Fast

If you find that your **battery is draining quickly**, it can be very frustrating. There are several reasons why this might happen, and here are some ways to fix it.

Solution:

- **Check Battery Usage**: Go to **Settings** > **Battery and Device Care** > **Battery**. This will show you which apps are using the most battery. If you notice that an app is using a lot of power, you can try limiting its background activity or uninstalling it if it's not needed.
- **Turn on Power Saving Mode**: You can extend your battery life by turning on **Power Saving Mode**. Go to **Settings** > **Battery and Device Care** > **Battery** > **Power Saving Mode**. This will limit some of the phone's background functions, saving power.
- **Disable Unnecessary Features**: Turn off features you're not using, such as **Bluetooth**, **Wi-Fi**, and **Location Services**. These can drain the battery even when not in use.
- **Reduce Screen Brightness**: If your screen is too bright, it will use more battery. You can enable **Adaptive Brightness**, which automatically adjusts the brightness based on your surroundings. Go to **Settings** > **Display** > **Adaptive Brightness** and turn it on.

2. Phone Running Slow

If you notice that your phone is getting **slower** over time, there are several steps you can take to speed it up.

Solution:

- **Clear Cache**: Apps store data in a cache to help them run faster, but over time, the cache can become too large and slow down the phone. To clear the cache, go to **Settings** > **Storage** > **Other Apps**. Here, you can select apps and clear their cache.
- **Uninstall Unnecessary Apps**: If you have apps that you don't use, uninstall them. Go to **Settings** > **Apps**, select the app, and tap **Uninstall**.
- **Close Background Apps**: If you have too many apps running in the background, it can slow down your phone. Swipe up from the bottom of the screen to see your open apps, and swipe them away to close them.
- **Perform a Software Update**: Samsung regularly releases updates to improve performance. Go to **Settings** > **Software Update** > **Download and Install** to make sure your phone is up to date.

3. Wi-Fi or Bluetooth Not Connecting

If your phone is having trouble connecting to Wi-Fi or Bluetooth devices, here are some steps you can take to fix it.

Solution:

- **Turn Off and On Wi-Fi/Bluetooth**: Sometimes, simply turning off and turning back on **Wi-Fi** or **Bluetooth** can fix connection issues. Swipe down from the top of the screen to open the Quick Settings panel, and toggle Wi-Fi or Bluetooth off and on.
- **Forget and Reconnect**: If you're having trouble connecting to a Wi-Fi network, go to **Settings** > **Connections** > **Wi-Fi**. Tap the network you're having trouble with, then tap **Forget**. After that, reconnect by selecting the network again and entering the password.
- **Reset Network Settings**: If the problem persists, you can reset your network settings. Go to **Settings** > **General Management** > **Reset** > **Reset Network Settings**. This will reset your Wi-Fi, Bluetooth, and mobile data settings.

4. Overheating

If your phone is getting **too hot** during use, it might be because you're running too many apps or using high-powered features for a long time, such as gaming or video streaming.

Solution:

- **Close Unnecessary Apps**: Close any apps that you aren't using. This will free up resources and prevent the phone from working harder than it needs to.
- **Use in a Cool Environment**: If you're using your phone in direct sunlight or in a hot environment, it might get too hot. Try to use it in a cooler area.
- **Turn Off Power-Hungry Features**: Features like **GPS**, **Bluetooth**, and **Wi-Fi** can use a lot of power. Turn them off if you don't need them.
- **Remove Case**: If you're using a case on your phone, it might be trapping heat. Try removing the case when using the phone for extended periods of time.

5. Touch Screen Not Responding

Sometimes, the **touch screen** on your phone might not respond as expected. This could be due to a variety of issues, such as a software glitch or physical obstruction.

Solution:

- **Clean the Screen**: Dirt, dust, and oils from your fingers can cause the screen to be less responsive. Use a soft cloth to gently clean the screen.
- **Restart the Phone**: A simple **restart** can often fix minor glitches. Hold down the power button and select **Restart**.
- **Check for Screen Protector Issues**: If you have a **screen protector**, make sure it is not interfering with the touch sensitivity. Try removing it to see if that helps.
- **Update Your Software**: Sometimes, software updates fix issues with the screen. Go to **Settings** > **Software Update** > **Download and Install** to check for updates.

11.2 How to Factory Reset and Backup

If your Galaxy S24 Ultra is still not working well after trying the solutions above, or if you want to start fresh, you might consider performing a **factory reset**. A factory reset will erase everything on your phone and restore it to its original settings. However, it's important to **back up** your data before doing a factory reset to avoid losing important files.

How to Back Up Your Data

Before performing a factory reset, make sure you back up your data, such as your contacts, photos, and apps. Samsung offers several ways to back up your data.

Solution 1: Use Samsung Cloud Samsung provides **Samsung Cloud**, which allows you to back up your data to their servers. To back up your data:

- Go to **Settings** > **Accounts and Backup** > **Backup and Restore**.
- Tap **Back Up Data**.
- Select the items you want to back up (such as apps, contacts, and photos) and tap **Back Up**.

Solution 2: Use Google Backup If you prefer using Google's services, you can back up your phone to your **Google Account**. To do this:

- Go to **Settings** > **Accounts and Backup** > **Google Backup**.
- Make sure **Back Up to Google Drive** is turned on.

- You can also back up specific items like your contacts and calendar.

Solution 3: Use External Storage You can also back up your data to an **SD card** or **external hard drive**. To do this:

- Connect your SD card or external storage device to your phone.
- Go to **Settings** > **Storage** and select **Transfer Data**.
- Choose the items you want to move to the external storage device.

Once your data is safely backed up, you can proceed with the **factory reset**.

How to Perform a Factory Reset

A **factory reset** will erase all the data on your phone, returning it to its original state. Here's how to do it:

Solution:

- Go to **Settings** > **General Management** > **Reset**.
- Tap **Factory Data Reset**.

- You will see a list of all the data that will be erased, including apps, contacts, photos, and settings.
- Tap **Reset** to confirm and enter your password or PIN.
- After that, tap **Delete All** to begin the factory reset.

The phone will restart and begin the reset process. Once it's complete, your phone will be restored to its original settings, as if it were brand new.

11.3 Frequently Asked Questions (FAQs)

Here are some of the most **frequently asked questions** about the **Samsung Galaxy S24 Ultra**, along with their answers.

1. How do I enable dark mode on the Galaxy S24 Ultra?

Answer: To enable **Dark Mode**, follow these steps:

- Go to **Settings** > **Display** > **Dark Mode**.
- Toggle the switch to turn it on.

Dark Mode reduces the brightness of your screen and uses darker colors, which can help save battery and be easier on your eyes, especially in low-light environments.

2. Can I use a microSD card with the Galaxy S24 Ultra?

Answer: No, the Galaxy S24 Ultra does not have a microSD card slot. You can, however, use cloud services like **Samsung Cloud** or **Google Drive** to store your files, or you can use **external storage devices** like USB drives or hard drives.

3. How do I take a screenshot on the Galaxy S24 Ultra?

Answer: To take a screenshot, press the **Volume Down** button and the **Power** button at the same time. Hold them for a moment, and your screen will flash to indicate the screenshot has been taken. You can find the screenshot in your **Gallery** app.

4. How do I unlock my Galaxy S24 Ultra with my face or fingerprint?

Answer: To enable **face recognition** or **fingerprint scanning**, go to **Settings** > **Biometrics and Security** >

Face Recognition or **Fingerprint**. Follow the on-screen instructions to set up the feature.

5. What should I do if my phone is not charging?

Answer: If your phone is not charging:

- Check that the charging cable and adapter are properly connected.
- Make sure the charging port on your phone is clean and free from dust.
- Try using a different charging cable or adapter to see if the issue is with the charger.
- If using a wireless charger, ensure that the charger is positioned correctly.

Conclusion

The **Samsung Galaxy S24 Ultra** is an amazing phone, but like any technology, it can sometimes run into problems. In this chapter, we've explored some **common issues** you may face, such as battery draining too fast, connectivity problems, and performance slowdowns, and provided **solutions** to fix them. We've also covered how to **backup** your data and perform a **factory reset** if needed. Finally, we've answered some of the most **frequently asked questions** to help you make the most of your phone.

If you follow these tips and solutions, you should be able to keep your Samsung Galaxy S24 Ultra running smoothly and enjoy using all its amazing features.

Final Verdict

The **Samsung Galaxy S24 Ultra** is one of the most advanced smartphones on the market. It has many features that make it stand out, such as a powerful camera system, a large and beautiful display, long battery life, and much more. However, like any product, it has both its **strengths** and **weaknesses**. In this chapter, we will take an in-depth look at the **pros** and **cons** of the Galaxy S24 Ultra to help you decide whether it's the right phone for you. We'll also discuss **who should buy the Galaxy S24 Ultra** and what kind of user will benefit most from this phone.

12.1 Pros and Cons of the Galaxy S24 Ultra

The Samsung Galaxy S24 Ultra is a high-end flagship device, so it comes with many features designed to provide top performance. However, as with any product, there are some areas where it excels and others where it could be improved. Let's go over the **pros** and **cons** to give you a clearer picture of what this phone offers.

Pros of the Galaxy S24 Ultra

1. **Stunning Display Quality**

One of the biggest strengths of the Galaxy S24 Ultra is its **display**. The phone comes with a **6.8-inch Dynamic AMOLED 2X** screen, which offers vibrant colors, deep blacks, and excellent brightness. The **Adaptive 120Hz refresh rate** makes scrolling and gaming incredibly smooth, providing a very enjoyable visual experience. The **HDR10+ support** enhances video content by offering better contrast, brightness, and color accuracy. Whether you are watching videos, playing games, or browsing photos, the display quality is one of the best available.

2. **Impressive Camera System**

The **camera system** is another standout feature of the Galaxy S24 Ultra. It boasts a **200MP primary camera**, which is among the highest-resolution cameras available in a smartphone. This allows for incredibly detailed photos, even when zoomed in. The **telephoto and periscope lenses** provide excellent zoom capabilities without sacrificing image quality. Whether you're taking portraits, landscapes, or close-up shots, the camera delivers impressive results. The **night mode** also ensures that your photos look good even in low-light conditions.

3. **5G Connectivity**

The **5G support** in the Galaxy S24 Ultra ensures that you get fast internet speeds wherever 5G networks are available. This means faster download speeds, smoother streaming, and better overall internet performance. If you're someone who uses their phone for heavy data activities, like downloading large files or streaming high-definition content, 5G is a huge benefit.

4. **Long Battery Life**

The **5000mAh battery** in the Galaxy S24 Ultra is more than enough to get you through the day with typical use. The phone can last a full day with a mix of tasks like browsing, social media, watching videos, and gaming. Additionally, **fast charging** and **wireless charging** ensure that you can charge your phone quickly when you do need to top up. The **battery life** is solid, especially for a phone with such powerful features.

5. **S Pen and Productivity Features**

The **S Pen** that comes with the Galaxy S24 Ultra adds an extra layer of productivity to the device. Whether you're taking notes, drawing, or controlling the phone with **Air Actions**, the S Pen is a great tool for both personal and professional use. If you need a phone that helps you stay productive on the go, the S Pen is a significant advantage.

6. Premium Design and Build Quality

The Galaxy S24 Ultra is made with **premium materials**, including **Corning Gorilla Glass Victus 2** on the front and back and an **aluminum frame**. The phone has a solid feel and looks elegant. It's a bit large, but it fits well in the hand, especially with its rounded edges. It's built to withstand the rigors of daily use, and the **IP68 rating** makes it resistant to water and dust.

7. One UI and Software Features

Samsung's **One UI** provides a smooth and user-friendly interface. It comes with many **customization options**, including features like **Edge Panels**, **Dark Mode**, and **Bixby Routines**. Samsung's software has a clean, easy-to-use design, and you get regular updates to improve performance and security.

Cons of the Galaxy S24 Ultra

1. High Price

One of the biggest drawbacks of the Galaxy S24 Ultra is its **price**. It is a **premium device**, and premium devices come with a premium price tag. If you're on a budget or if you don't need all the high-end features, the S24 Ultra might be more expensive than what you need. While the phone's performance justifies the price for many users, it can be a tough choice for those who are looking for more affordable options.

2. **Large Size May Be Difficult to Handle**

The Galaxy S24 Ultra has a **large screen** (6.8 inches), which is great for watching videos and gaming, but it can be **difficult to handle** for people with smaller hands. It may be challenging to use one-handed, especially for tasks like typing or reaching the top of the screen. Samsung offers a **One-Handed Mode**, but it's still not the most comfortable phone to use with just one hand.

3. **No MicroSD Card Slot**

Unlike some of Samsung's older models, the **Galaxy S24 Ultra** does not have a **microSD card slot**. This means you can't expand the storage with an SD card. While the phone offers plenty of internal storage options (up to **1TB**), you might still miss the ability to add more storage with an SD card, especially if you store a lot of photos, videos, or apps.

4. **No Headphone Jack**

Like many modern smartphones, the Galaxy S24 Ultra **does not have a headphone jack**. If you like using wired headphones, you'll need to use a **USB-C to headphone jack adapter** or switch to **wireless headphones**. Many users have moved to Bluetooth headphones, but if you still prefer wired ones, this could be an inconvenience.

5. **No Major Design Changes**

While the design of the Galaxy S24 Ultra is sleek and premium, it's not much different from its predecessors. If you're upgrading from a previous **Galaxy Ultra model**, the design may feel quite similar. The **camera bump** is slightly more pronounced, but overall, the changes in appearance are minimal.

6. **Limited Customization for Software**

While **One UI** is a great interface, it still has some limitations compared to **stock Android**. Some users may feel that they can't fully customize the phone's look and feel to their liking. If you prefer a more **customizable Android experience**, other devices may offer more flexibility.

7. **Heavy for Some Users**

The Galaxy S24 Ultra is **heavier** than many other smartphones. Weighing over **230 grams**, it's a substantial device. While this weight adds to the premium feel, it might be uncomfortable for users who prefer lighter devices. If you carry your phone in your pocket or hold it for extended periods, the weight might become noticeable.

12.2 Who Should Buy the Galaxy S24 Ultra?

The Samsung Galaxy S24 Ultra is a **premium phone** packed with features, but it may not be the right choice for everyone. So, who should consider buying the Galaxy S24 Ultra? Let's take a look at the types of users who will benefit most from this device.

1. Power Users Who Need Top Performance

If you are someone who needs the **best performance** for heavy tasks like gaming, video editing, or multitasking, the Galaxy S24 Ultra is an excellent choice. With its **Snapdragon 8 Gen 3 processor, 12GB of RAM**, and **200MP camera**, it can handle anything you throw at it without slowing down. Whether you are working on demanding apps or enjoying high-end mobile games, this phone will perform at the highest level.

2. Photography Enthusiasts

If you enjoy **photography** and want a phone that takes stunning photos, the **200MP camera** and the other advanced lenses (telephoto, ultra-wide, and periscope) will give you the tools you need to capture incredible shots. Whether you're a casual photographer or an enthusiast who likes to experiment with camera settings, the Galaxy S24 Ultra offers a wide range of options to help you take amazing photos in all kinds of lighting.

3. Media Lovers and Gamers

If you love watching videos or playing mobile games, the **large 6.8-inch display** with **HDR10+ support** and the **120Hz refresh rate** will make everything look amazing. The high-quality display, combined with the **stereo speakers** and **5G connectivity**, provides an outstanding media experience. Gamers will appreciate the fast performance and smooth graphics, while movie lovers will enjoy the vivid colors and sharp detail.

4. People Who Want a Premium Experience

If you appreciate **premium design** and **cutting-edge technology**, the Galaxy S24 Ultra will meet your expectations. The phone is made with high-quality materials, including **Gorilla Glass Victus 2** and an **aluminum frame**, and it has a sleek, modern look. For users who want a phone that feels luxurious and sophisticated, the S24 Ultra is an excellent choice.

5. Professionals Who Need Productivity Features

For professionals who need to stay productive on the go, the **S Pen** and the **Samsung DeX** feature are huge advantages. Whether you are taking notes, creating presentations, or working on documents, the S Pen makes your work more efficient. The ability to connect the phone to a monitor using **Samsung DeX** turns the S24 Ultra into a portable workstation.

Conclusion

The Samsung Galaxy S24 Ultra is a **powerful and premium device** with many standout features, such as an incredible **camera system**, **amazing display**, and **fast 5G connectivity**. It offers excellent performance, a great user experience, and many productivity tools, making it a perfect choice for

power users, **photographers**, **gamers**, and those who want a **premium experience**.

However, it's important to consider the **high price** and the **large size**, which might not be suitable for everyone. If you prefer a lighter, more affordable phone or don't need all the advanced features, there are other options available.

If you are looking for the best of the best, the **Samsung Galaxy S24 Ultra** is a top choice. It's a phone that excels in almost every category, offering a premium experience that will satisfy those who want the most powerful features available in a smartphone.

www.ingramcontent.com/pod-product-compliance
Lightning Source LLC
LaVergne TN
LVHW051659050326
832903LV00032B/3910